**The RIGHT DEGREE FOR ME**

# WHAT DEGREE DO I NEED TO PURSUE A CAREER IN BUSINESS?

TAMRA ORR

ROSEN
PUBLISHING®

Published in 2015 by The Rosen Publishing Group, Inc.
29 East 21st Street, New York, NY 10010

First Edition

**Library of Congress Cataloging-in-Publication Data**

Orr, Tamra.
What degree do I need to pursue a career in business?/Tamra B. Orr.
        pages cm.—(The right degree for me)
Audience: Grades 7–12.
Includes bibliographical references and index.
ISBN 978-1-4777-7853-1 (library bound)
1. Business education—Vocational guidance—Juvenile literature. I. Title.
HF1106.O77 2015
650.071'1—dc23

                                          2014012403

*Manufactured in the United States of America*

# CONTENTS

The world of business is an exciting one, from stepping through the front door of one of America's top department stores as a customer—this striking space is a Macy's in Chicago, Illinois—to sitting behind a corporate desk as an employee.

# INTRODUCTION

**H**ey, have you ever thought about going into business?"

Have you been asked this question before? If so, it wouldn't be surprising if you felt too confused to respond properly. After all, what is business? Isn't every company a business? Doesn't it cover everything from the corner gas station and mega-chain department store to the mom-and-pop-owned secondhand thrift shop and Forbes 500 executive companies?

In a word, yes, all of those are businesses. So how in the world do you know if you want to go into business?

If you are confused, it's understandable. The term "business" has multiple meanings, but when it comes to a career pathway, it refers to "an organization engaging in commercial, industrial, or professional activities, whether for profit or nonprofit."

Chances are, you've been dealing with some form of business all of your life. When you started a lawn-mowing service or delivered newspapers, you were in business. When you worked at the local fast-food restaurant, you worked for a business. When you helped your parents send out mass e-mails for their store's latest sale, you helped a business.

So, what does it really mean to "go into business"?

It means choosing a career that will immerse you in providing a service or product to the public, whether directly or indirectly. Unlike some professions, business is made up of many different areas of study. It can be focused on:

- Accounting
- Finance
- Marketing
- Human resource management
- Management sciences
- Economics
- Computer sciences
- Entrepreneurship/small business
- Real estate
- Retail
- Sales
- Consulting

Clearly, "going into business" covers a huge variety of interests. How do you know in which direction you should go? Start by asking yourself some important questions. Don't answer them quickly, either. Take your time, and go back to some of them when new responses occur to you.

1. *Do you enjoy working with people?* If so, how many? Are you comfortable with a few? Can

you easily talk to and communicate with many new people on a daily basis? These questions are essential to consider so that if you do go into business, you choose wisely between a job that would make you part of a small business or team—or one that would put you at the front lines of selling and marketing, dealing with countless customers.

2. *Do you enjoy working with numbers?* If so, how much? Virtually every element of business is going to involve a great deal of number manipulating. Whether you're just filling out your tax forms or figuring out payroll for a small group, or you're the head of accounting for a huge corporation or tabulating sales reports for the year, handling numbers is bound to play a large role in your job.

3. *How are your overall communication skills?* Can you write clearly and concisely? Can you speak in front of people and negotiate or mediate when necessary? From the interoffice memo to the annual presentation to the investors, your ability to string together words will be tested daily in the world of business. In addition, you might be called on to mediate problems with staff or negotiate solutions for unhappy customers.

4. *How well can you network and sell yourself?* Are you computer and social media savvy? You have to be in today's global marketplace. You will also have to be able to "toot your own

horn" as they say. In other words, you have to be comfortable reminding people that you, your product, or your service are something they want and need! Sometimes this interaction will be face-to-face, but more often, it is via online and social media site networking.

5. *Are you competitive?* Businesses that don't compete don't survive. You will be expected to further a business in one way or another, and that often means competing to get the better price, better product, better campaign, or better cost. If battling to be the one on top is an exhilarating—not intimidating—idea, you're heading in the right direction.

6. *Are you creative?* Don't be misled into thinking creativity is important only to philosophy and English majors. Anyone in business must be extremely creative in order to succeed. Being in any field of business will require you to be imaginative and inventive in order to help solve problems and brainstorm solutions and ideas.

Once you've considered these questions and you feel you're still well suited for a career in business, the next question will be what type—and what kind of education will you need to get there? To determine that, you will need to answer a few more questions:

1. What type of business interests you the most?

2. Can you open your own business?
3. What time frame works best for you (weeks to years)?
4. What program is best for your interests—a certificate, an associate's degree, a bachelor's degree, or even an MBA (master's degree in business)?

To figure out the answers to these questions, read on.

# CHAPTER ONE

# When Everything Is Your Business

**W**hat do Subway sandwich restaurants, Facebook, and WordPress all have in common? All three of them are extremely successful businesses, and each one was started by a teenager.

WordPress is considered one of the easiest and most powerful blogging systems today, and it was started by teenager Matthew Mullenweg, now a millionaire-plus!

Do you have an incredible idea for a new product? Do you offer a service that is unlike any other one you know of? Perhaps you would really like to go into business, but for yourself, rather than for someone else.

If so, congratulations! There is little doubt that you have plenty of initiative, imagination, and determination. Unfortunately, those qualities alone are rarely enough to result in success.  Starting your own business, especially when you are young and do not have a lot of experience, is not easy. Having the idea is a great start, but there are many steps between your original concept and cash in the bank.

In an article published by the Association of Specialized and Cooperative Library Agencies, the author addresses some of the most commonly asked questions about opening a small business. The article states, "You will be your own most important asset, so an objective appraisal of your strengths and weaknesses is essential." Do you know what your strengths and weaknesses are? Try making a list (business-related), and then ask your friends and family for their input.

## Making Plans

Going into business on your own requires a detailed plan defining precisely what you plan to do, how you will do it, and what it will require. The plan acts as a guide or a map for you, detailing what resources you have (and need), what money is on hand and what will need to be borrowed (if any), and how it will be repaid. In addition, having a business often involves legal elements as well. You will need to learn about licenses, permits, zoning laws, and other local regulations. You will have to get familiar with the basics of bookkeeping, record keeping, and accounting. You will also need to understand income tax, tax rates, and tax forms.

Going into business for yourself often requires hours of online research in order to understand the details of putting together a business plan from start to finish.

You will need to find additional tips and resources on how to best market and advertise your business.

Sample business plans and templates are available online to help you flesh out the details of your business plan. Below, you'll find an overview of what goes into the standard business plan. Even if you do not use it for starting your own business, you will see a great deal of this form in business classes. Learning how it is created will help you look at every business differently and more analytically.

## General Business Plan Basics

The first section will be a summary listing the key concepts that will be described in detail in the rest of the plan. One or two sentences will

## MEETING MILLIONAIRES

Need a little inspiration to pursue your business dreams? Check out some of these young people whose determination and talent made them incredibly successful:

*Leanna Archer/Leanna's Hair:* At nine, Leanna took her grandmother's secret formula for hair pomade and began selling it to her friends. At age nineteen, she became the CEO of her company of all-natural hair products and established the Leanna Arch Education Foundation to help build schools in Haiti.

*Robert Nay/Nay Games:* In 2011, a fourteen-year-old with no coding experience spent a lot of time at the library researching. Soon, he produced *Bubble Ball*, a mobile game app that has sold more than a million downloads from the Apple app store.

Creating a business or product often grows out of your personal interests and abilities. What do you excel at that could be turned into a career?

Robert Nay's company, Nay Games, has released an additional twenty-four levels of the game.

*Nick D'Aloisio/Summly:* As a teen, Nick created an app that summarizes news articles for the iPhone. By age fifteen, he had financial backing from Horizon Ventures, and in March 2013, he sold his company to Yahoo! for $30 million.

*Sean Belnick/Bizchair.com:* At age fourteen, Sean started an online furniture company with nothing more than an idea and $500. In 2004, he opened a warehouse. In 2009, he expanded it. In 2010, profits topped $58 million.

be enough for defining your business's objectives, product/service offerings, reasons for success, projected growth and market, other team members (if any), and funding details.

The second section is typically products/services. This is where you will answer why there is a need for your business, what makes your product/service unique, how it will compete with similar products/services (if any), what kind of pricing you will implement, and what obstacles you will have to face to put the product/service on the market.

The third section is the market. This section focuses on who your market is, how your product/service will be priced, and to what kind of customers you plan to appeal.

Next, you will focus on the best marketing strategy for your business. Possible options include social media, a website, TV, radio, print, direct mail, telephone sales, one-on-one sales, and word of mouth.

You should include a section on competition in the marketplace. Who has a product/service like yours? How are they the same or different? How is your business better?

Operations is the next section, with details on how you will manufacture or produce your product/service, what equipment you will need, and how you will get it all. This is followed by information about your team or personnel—any people who will be in the business with you and what their job responsibilities will be.

The final section is where financial data is detailed. Topics covered here include income statements, cash flow information, and balance sheets. Often business plans are supported by a variety of documents, including your résumé, quotes/estimates, information on prospective customers, and legal documents.

Feeling overwhelmed yet? That's understandable. All of this work can be intimidating, but don't give up on your great idea just yet. Who knows? You may be the next Fred DeLuca (Subway), Mark Zuckerberg (Facebook), or Matt Mullenweg (WordPress).

# Finding Information

There are many free resources that help you figure out everything. You can start with local organizations such as your city or town's branch of the chamber of commerce and the Small Business Administration (SBA). You can also learn a great deal from career counselors

# A COMBINATION OF MOTIVATION AND ENTHUSIASM

Jacob Schroeder just might turn out to be one of tomorrow's millionaire teens. While he was growing up in New Mexico, he worked as a reporter for Scholastic News, getting the chance to interview not only New Mexico governors but also U.S. senator John McCain and even President Barack Obama. In addition to his reporting, Jacob helped his mother with her children's event company, learning how to twist balloons for young people at large educational community events.

Jacob and his family moved to Oregon, and he continued twisting balloons at area farmers' markets. In early 2013, he started a business called Imagine Balloons. "It is a balloon twisting entertainment company that offers imaginative balloons and fun carnival games," he explained in a personal interview. "I can twist whatever my customers can imagine out of balloons. Kids love the different designs, and I make sure that no matter what, the product will make their day!" Currently, Jacob is twisting on a weekly basis and is working to expand from local venues to birthday parties and holiday events.

The original motivation behind Jacob's business came from a good friend and foreign exchange student named Shohta. Jacob was hoping to save up

(continued on page 19)

Jacob Schroeder, a kid reporter for Scholastic News, interviewed Republican presidential candidate Senator John McCain in Albuquerque, New Mexico, in 2008. From there, his entrepreneurial bent ballooned.

(*continued from page 17*)

enough money to visit Shohta in Japan when his friend was diagnosed with leukemia. "When I heard the news, I was determined to get enough money to visit him when he finished his chemo treatments," explained Jacob. He hopes to go to Japan after Shohta recovers from his bone marrow transplant. In addition to saving up for the trip, Jacob is also earning money for his future college fund. "I've had a lot of offers to twist for birthday parties and special events," said Jacob. "I've had a lot of success so far!"

Jacob promotes Imagine Balloons by handing out brochures and business cards. "I also have a cart where I post designs and prices," he added. "I have a lot of repeat customers." So far, Jacob's main investor is his mom. "She helped me out by buying me some balloons, but now I buy most of my supplies out of my profits. In addition to money, she also invests her time by hanging around at big events to help me with technical things—like making sure my umbrella doesn't blow away."

In 2014, at the age of fifteen, Jacob was already looking ahead to the future. "I look forward to owning my own company when I'm an adult," he said. "As our world is changing rapidly, our society's needs will change, and the type of business I start will be based on those needs—and market research. I am quite enthusiastic as I think it is a key to success," he added. "I am motivated, a hard worker, and creative—which is the key to being an entrepreneur."

at your school, at career centers, and in school and public libraries. The Internet is a vast resource as well, and you can find helpful information by just doing a quick search.

The Small Business Administration is an excellent place to begin your search about starting a business. This user-friendly website offers free online videos, classes, resource guides, and much more. The SBA

One of the best resources for your business idea is your family. Getting your family's support may be what you need to turn a good idea into a successful business.

has focused on aiding, counseling, assisting, and protecting small businesses since it began in 1953.

The SBA website offers information on starting and managing a business, the technicalities and complexities of loans and grants, and the lowdown on contracting issues. A few of the free online courses offered to those interested in a career in business include: Business Technology Simplified, Cybersecurity for Small Businesses, Encore Entrepreneurs: An Introduction to Starting Your Own Business, and How to Write a Business Plan.

Of course, some of best ideas, support, encouragement, and possible investments can come from your family. Talk over your ideas with your parents and siblings. Get their input and have them sit in and contribute to any of your brainstorming sessions. According to the financial literacy website She Counts, talking to your parents can be surprisingly helpful: "You may not only find a couple of willing investors for your enterprise, you will also gain knowledge, insight, and guidance from folks who might have 'been there, done that' and can give you the benefit of their experience."

# CHAPTER TWO

# Get Ready... a Business Career Through Certificates

When it comes to certificates, there is definitely good news and bad news. First, the good news. There are many business-related certificates from which to choose. They are usually affordable, so there are no worries about tracking down scholarships, loans, and grants. Certificates can be earned quickly (often in a matter of weeks or less). Certifications help make your résumé stand out from others. Some certifications are enough to get you hired at the entry level and working as you decide to either pursue additional education or realize that perhaps business is not the right career path for you. You can earn a certificate while still working full-time, and if your current job is already related to business, earning a certificate may also earn you a raise or a stronger chance for promotion.

And now, here is the bad news. A certificate alone is most likely not going to gain you the job with the big bucks. It will get you in the door and gain you experience and skill, but, as you will see as you read

Often the first step into the business world is as a receptionist or front-desk worker. Taking such a position provides a great opportunity to observe the roles and responsibilities around you.

through this book, the business jobs that are growing the fastest and are in the most demand tend to require a degree. If you think about it, that makes sense. Training that takes only a few months and a few hundred dollars is not likely to earn you the same paycheck as an education that takes four or more years and thousands of dollars.

Certificate series courses, often also referred to as workforce development, range in price and duration depending on the subject and the individual school. Some are taught face-to-face, while others are done online. Some of the business-related certifications available include:

- Administrative assistant
- Business intelligence
- Business mediation
- Human resources management
- Marketing brand management
- Marketing project
- Project management
- Training and development
- Workplace communication skills

## Certification Up Close and Personal

Let's take a closer look at a few of these courses and see what is involved in completing them. (Please note that each school offering these classes may vary in one or more ways.)

## Administrative Assistant Certification

These courses are designed to help you learn how to efficiently use all of the most common office tools. They

If working on the computer, dealing with documents, and shuffling papers—even if they are digital—appeals to you, becoming an administrative assistant can be a great step.

focus on basic communication skills and organization tips, from filing systems to online usage and research. First, you will likely take the core classes about administrative office procedures, workplace behaviors, correspondence and communication, and Internet research. After that, you can choose from elective courses in computer technology, including multiple levels of the widely used Microsoft Word, PowerPoint, Outlook, Excel, or Access. At completion of this course, you will likely be able to approach an employer with a certificate as a trained administrative assistant.

# Business Mediation Certification

Mediation is defined as "the functions of an impartial third party in assisting two or more disputing parties to reach a self-determined and mutually acceptable solution to a problem that requires the consent of the parties to become actionable." This certification gives you the education and skills you would need to become a neutral third-party, court-appointed mediator. Courses typically include an introduction to mediation, mediation in the workplace, conflict and problem-solving strategies, and negotiation practices. Students will likely spend time analyzing case studies and role-playing mediation scenarios. At the completion of the course, students are given an exam.

# Project Management Certification

This series of courses helps workers learn the skills of managing a successful project, including proper sequence of actions, control of costs, and effective follow-through. Courses typically include an introduction to project management, integration and scope management, time management and cost management, human resource and quality management, communications and risk management, and procurement and stakeholder management. Depending on which school you choose,

## LEARNING SOMETHING NEW EVERY DAY

Debra McClaughry decided she wanted to start her own personal training studio in Salem, Oregon. She knew that getting the right certificates would make it easier to help her clients. As she explained in a personal interview, first, she became certified in first aid, CPR, and AED (automatic external defibrillator). Later, she earned her certification as a certified personal trainer (CPT). "I enjoy helping people and love training myself and others," she said. "It was absolutely the right decision for me at this point in my life. I love what I do and seeing people accomplish something they thought they couldn't." McClaughry applies her training on a daily basis and feels like she learns something new each and every day. "Really examine your self-motivation, drive, and ambition levels," she advised. "Make sure you are doing it for the love of what you do, and not for the money. Money is helpful, but loving what you do is so much more important in the long run."

there are many levels of this type of certificate. For example, the Project Management Institute offers six levels, depending on your preferences and prior experience. You can find out the differences among each type at the institute's website.

## Marketing Project Certification

Effective marketing is often the key to selling a product or service, whether it is one you came up with and want to sell or the next one in the product line of a huge company. This course focuses on showing you the techniques to efficient marketing so that people know about the product/service, what it does, and why they need to have it. Courses typically include marketing principles, marketing and business management, developing a marketing plan, and marketing on the Internet.

## Workplace Communication Skills Certification

This more advanced course is designed to help students develop and improve their English skills for use in the workplace. It offers lessons on both written and spoken communication. Courses typically include communication improvement, accent modification, advanced grammar, advanced conversation, presentation skills for the workplace, writing skills for the workplace, and reading and vocabulary comprehension.

## Lessons at Lunch

Lunchtime is usually your chance to get something to eat, relax, read, listen to music, or chat with other people. In recent years, some companies, schools, and community centers have also started offering lunchtime certificate programs. These classes allow you to eat, drink—and learn.

Topics change from one company to the next, as does the length and duration of the classes. At Texas's Collin College, for example, the school offers a lunchtime certificate series in two business courses: Leadership Tools for Success and Project Management: An Overview. Over the course of twelve to twenty hours, participants can

Collin College in Plano, Texas, is a beautiful place to pause, munch, and learn while you're at it.

learn a great deal and end up with a certificate to add to their résumés and portfolios. Ask your employer or school for possible opportunities for these classes.

## Out of the Box

If you're interested in certifications but want to find something a little more specific to your interests, you might want to explore courses in landscape, education, interior design, or wedding and event planning. A certificate in wine business management from Sonoma State University, for example, is offered online at three levels. It focuses on e-commerce, supply chain management, wine marketing and sales, quality management, and other business issues involved in winemaking and viticulture.

Getting a certificate can be one of the wisest career choices you can make. Whether or not you go directly into business, many of these classes can help boost your résumé above the rest, plus give you skills you will need in virtually every work situation. In addition, certification can show employers you're serious about being a strong and essential employee.

Earning a certificate displays ambition and drive to both current and future employers.

# FULL-TIME

Michelle Bergeron works hard to find enough hours in her day to get everything done. Living in Idaho, Bergeron is a full-time student, full-time worker, and full-time single mom to her young son. At her job at a call center, she took over when her project manager fell ill. "I told her to relax and tell me what to do," she recalled in a personal interview. "That day made me feel invigorated—I loved that position. I never thought I would find my dream career while filling in for someone."

Since then, Bergeron has been working in management and enjoying every minute of it. At the age of twenty-six, Bergeron began working toward her associate's degree in business leadership at North Idaho College. The degree will include a project leader certificate. "Business leadership means I don't have to take other classes, but just accounting, IT, data management, and so on. I am hoping this degree will help me gain a position as a project manager," she said. "I am doing this in order to follow my dreams and show my son that no matter what obstacle or bump there may be on your road of life, you can achieve anything as long as you're determined. Just have drive—and a willingness to learn."

Certificate classes can introduce you to business slowly and help you determine if such a career choice is the best one for you. Certification can get your foot in the door of a company that may be willing to help you pursue additional education, or it may be the deciding factor in your pay rate when hired. Generally speaking, certificate classes are short and relatively inexpensive, so check into what options are available today. Who knows where those classes might take you tomorrow?

# CHAPTER THREE

# Get Set...a Business Career Through an Associate's Degree

**G**etting an associate's degree in business is the perfect middle-of-the-road option for some people—it takes longer and costs more than a certificate, but it also opens far more job opportunities. An associate's degree does not demand the commitment of a four-year bachelor's program, taking two years or less to complete. One of the greatest advantages of this type of degree is that you can often take courses while maintaining a full-time work schedule, especially if you choose to take an online course.

An associate's degree in business teaches core requirements for the first

Obtaining a degree online is one of the fastest -growing educational options today. Learning can be tailored to individual needs and preferences.

## ROLES ON THE RISE

Working as an administrative assistant might just be one of the best possible career choices you can make, according to the U.S. Department of Labor's Bureau of Labor Statistics. Office administrative services have been identified as one of the fastest-growing jobs for the next decade. Becoming a skilled and efficient assistant in the manufacturing, financial services, commercial real estate, and health care fields could result in increasing pay every year.

What qualities do hiring managers look for in their administrative assistants? Topping the list are organizational skills, initiative, and attention to detail. Those traits are followed by experience, job stability, adaptability, flexibility, superior technical skills, a commitment to continuing education, and interpersonal skills.

year and specialized business classes in the second. You will be introduced to a broad overview of:

- Business communications
- Sales and marketing
- Accounting
- Business law
- Management principles
- Information technology

While each school is going to vary, let's look at what you would likely study to earn an associate's degree in business management. This particular program typically requires around sixty hours.

First, there are approximately eighteen hours of general education requirements, which typically include three hours each of:

- English
- Business communications
- Economics I and II
- Math
- Elective courses

Next, students typically are required to take twenty-four hours of core business courses, three each in:

- Financial Accounting
- Managerial Accounting
- Introduction to Computing
- Introduction to Business
- Personal Finance
- Organization and Management
- Principles of Marketing
- Business Seminar
-

Finally, there are usually eighteen hours of business management courses, which include

- Business Communication
- Business Entrepreneurship
- Management of Human Resources

- Labor Relations Management
- Two three-hour business electives

## Online or Not?

Deciding whether to take courses online or on campus is not always an easy decision. Without a doubt, on-line classes have a number of benefits. You can take

Does getting an online degree appeal to you? What benefits can you see to it rather than not having to sit in class?

them at whatever times and days work best for you, arranging them around your work and family schedule. Most materials are accessible 24/7 from virtually any computer connection. You can move at your own pace, speeding up and slowing down as you need. Online classes tend to cost less, and many materials are available to download for free. Perhaps best of all, there is no time spent commuting in lousy weather or long lines of traffic.

While you might not be able to complete your entire degree online, you can do a great deal of the coursework and finish the rest in night classes or classes that meet for several hours once a week.

Before enrolling in any online program, you should ask several important questions. You can do this in an e-mail or phone interview.

1. Is the school accredited, and if so, by whom? If not, when might it be reviewed?
2. How long has the school existed, and how many students are currently enrolled? How many have graduated?
3. How much is tuition, and what does that figure include—and not include?
4. What education and experience do the majority of your teachers have?
5. How many students does a teacher work with on average?
6. What computer equipment/hardware/software is required for the courses?
7. What degrees are offered, and how long does it take to complete each program?

8. Are the programs flexible so that you can rush ahead or slow down, depending on your personal pace?
9. What curriculum is used, and what textbooks, if any, will need to be purchased?
10. What resources are available if you need extra help or have questions? How can you get in contact with the school or teachers if necessary?

Online programs are definitely convenient, but they're not perfect. It is much easier to procrastinate (and ignore) assignments when there is no one around to remind (and nag) you to meet the deadlines. "The biggest disadvantage of distance learning is the need to keep yourself motivated and disciplined," states an online article on the topic. "Unlike a traditional college, distance learning requires that students set their own schedule and find the time to do the work themselves. Many people find that without a schedule to keep them on track, they lack the discipline to get the work done."

Taking online classes can also feel lonely as the interaction of students and teachers who are face-to-face is missing. As an article on the website bgiedu.net states, "Many of those that attend online classes may find that they feel isolated. They may feel as if they are the only ones having problems with learning the material since there are no other students that they can talk to about the problem that they are having like after class at many traditional classrooms."

# Careers Up Close and Personal

An associate's degree can help you get at least an entry-level job in any of the following careers:

- Accounts payable clerk
- Accounts receivable clerk
- Administrative assistant
- Business analyst
- Customer service representative
- Finance officer
- Human resources assistant
- Junior accountant
- Loan officer
- Marketing specialist
- Sales representative
- Real estate agent
- Tax preparer

There are a number of different directions you can take with an associate's degree in business. Let's explore a couple of them a little closer.

## Administrative Assistant

Just as today's flight attendants were once called stewardesses, yesterday's secretaries are now often referred to as administrative assistants. Without an efficient and skilled assistant working behind the scenes, a number of high-powered offices and companies would fall apart. Administrative assistants file documents, draft messages, schedule appointments, and provide support for the rest of the staff. In addition, most assistants do their share of customer service for the company's clients.

Colleen Davie-Janes has held many different jobs, from actress to stand-up comedian, but she says she has relied on her skills as an administrative assistant to pay the bills. In an article on the Wall Street Services website, she explained that in her job at a top investment bank, she processes travel and expense reports, provides support to a staff of up to forty people, and creates various presentations. "My best advice for anyone pursuing a career as an Administrative Assistant," she wrote, "is to be very focused, have an amazing memory, really love helping people out, have unending patience, and be able to work with some incredibly difficult personalities. Approach each day as a fun challenge." She added, "What I love about being an admin is the non-stop action and the myriad of personalities. . . I just really enjoy the human interaction. It is NEVER boring. The hardest part of being an admin is that you are a helper, you are customer service, and as such, there's no time for being down, or grumpy, or having a bad day. It's your job to make everyone else's day easier, so suck it up and smile!"

- Expected job growth between now and 2020: 12 percent
- Possible spin-offs: receptionist, executive secretary, virtual assistant (working from home, via the Internet)

# Customer Service Representative

As a customer service representative, you are the face of a company. This position gives your job a great deal of power. You are the primary connection between a business and the customer, and it is your job to respond to complaints, requests, orders, and questions over the phone or via e-mail. This role entails strong written and spoken communication skills as well as the ability to listen attentively and respond professionally. If you do not perform your job well, there is no such thing as customer satisfaction, and without it, companies cannot survive for long.

Glen Kamps, store manager for Dick Pond Athletics in Illinois and a former customer service rep, told the *U.S. News* website, "Those who go above and beyond change people's lives. It's important for someone to have energy, a sense of humor, have a passion for helping people, good eye contact,

As the voice on the telephone is often a customer's sole representation of a company, it is an important one.

and a good attitude. When a person comes in, they are stuck in a problem and want to know what to do," he added. "We're problem solvers and teachers and are trying to help people."

- Expected job growth between now and 2020: 15 percent
- Possible spin-offs: call center representative, account manager, and customer service specialist

## Sales Representative

The job of a sales representative is to sell products or services to other businesses, government agencies, organizations, and consumers. This job calls on strong interpersonal communication skills, as well as being able to negotiate and sell over the computer, the phone, or in person. A number of sales reps are also required to keep close track of market conditions and what the competitors are doing.

In an interview with the *Wall Street Journal* online, Angela Holbrook, a recruiting manager for J.R. Simplot, a food and agribusiness company, said, "Being in sales is truly more about the relationships and the people. You also have to stay abreast on the newest techniques, communicate well, and know how to ask probing questions."

- Expected job growth between now and 2020: 16 percent
- Possible spin-offs: outside and inside sales representative, account manager

Learning how to prepare taxes is one way to make April an easier month for many people. Since taxes are unavoidable, jobs are usually plentiful!

## Tax Preparer

There is an old saying that only two things in life are truly inevitable: death and taxes. This means, as a tax preparer, you will most likely always have a job. Tax preparers often work in a variety of places, from small companies to huge corporations. This job

## CLIMBING HIGHER

Taryn Van Ausdell thought she knew what she wanted to do from the time she was seven years old. She enrolled in Oregon State University with a plan to major in engineering, she explained in an interview with the author. "I decided science wasn't for me," she said, "and so I returned to Portland and began working in a bank." It was while she was there that she realized something important. "People don't understand finances," she explained, "and that's when I decided I should go into accounting." This time she enrolled in Eastern Oregon University at the Mt. Hood Community College campus and completed her bachelor's degree.

Since then, Van Ausdell has been in the financial industry for a decade, training new and existing bank employees on how to be personal bankers and obtain additional skills. "Learning business-related information is exceptionally helpful in most industries," she said. "The things I have learned through obtaining my degree are helpful in life and business, and I would recommend this pathway to anyone. When I eventually apply for other positions at my bank, the higher I climb the more important it will be to have that degree on my résumé," she added. "Many positions would be closed to me if I did not have that degree—and I am very proud of it."

entails reviewing financial documents and records, completing tax returns, reviewing income and deductions, and working to keep each client's taxes as low as possible. Clearly, it requires a strong background in math, plus a good deal of customer service skills.

Tax work can be seasonal, with the main push being between January and May. Companies such as H&R Block and Jackson Hewitt hire thousands of tax professionals to work with them during these months. You can learn the basics in classes lasting six to twelve weeks. This measured approach can be a great way to discover if being a tax preparer is something you want to pursue in college. "The best thing about this job is the flexibility it offers," said Kathy Burlison, director of tax implementation for H&R Block. In an interview for Monster.com, she added, "We're looking for talented individuals with strong people skills who have some flexibility in their schedules, who can work days, weekends, or evenings."

- Expected job growth between now and 2020: 10 percent
- Possible spin-offs: tax consultant, income tax preparer, tax specialist

An associate's degree is an excellent introduction to business and the directions it can take you. It often helps you find the exact job you've been searching for or gets you the credits and foundation you need to go on to a four-year degree.

# CHAPTER FOUR

# Go! A Business Career Through a Bachelor's Degree

**G**etting a certificate or earning an associate's degree is often enough to get you in the business job you wanted. However, for some jobs or to be promoted at your company, a four-year bachelor's degree in business is often the best choice. This type of degree is just what you would expect—it takes longer and costs more. It also opens the door to higher-paying jobs and wider opportunities. For example, a bachelor's degree in business can lead to jobs in:

- Accounting
- Economics
- Entrepreneurship
- Finance
- General business
- Health care management
- Hospitality management
- Informational technology management
- International business

- Management
- Nonprofit management
- Operations management
- Project management
- Public relations
- Real estate
- Supply chain management

A career in real estate is one of the most interesting paths for a business career, especially if you're a people person. What's more, job opportunities are everywhere: from small towns to huge cities.

The first two years of the bachelor's degree are spent completing forty-two hours of core requirements, like:

- Business Communications and Critical Thinking
- Introduction to Computer Applications and Systems
- Management Theory and Practice
- Principles of Accounting
- Principles of Marketing
- Business Research and Law
- Principles of Microeconomics and Macroeconomics
- Finance for Business
- Global Business Strategies
- Social and Ethical Issues
- Organizational Theory, Behavior, and Management
- Business Statistics

An additional twenty-four credit hours are typically required in classes on commercial law, economics, money and banking, consumer behavior, and technical writing. During the third year, you will likely focus on more specific courses, depending on the area of business in which you plan to specialize.

## Careers Up Close and Personal

Now, let's take a look at some of the career paths that will likely be available to you when you have a four-year business degree.

# APPROACHABLE AND COACHABLE

When it comes to education and certification in business, few people have as many credentials on their résumés as John Holbrook. By age fifty-one, he earned a bachelor's degree in management and a master's degree in business administration, plus certifications in everything from processing and flow technologies to auditing and scheduling. Currently, he is putting his skills and experience to work as a continuous improvement specialist in the state of Washington. "My personal decisions to obtain professional certifications have greatly helped me find positions in our current credential-crazy environment," he said in a personal interview with the author. "Multiple forms of education and professional certifications add to your ability to be interviewed and possibly land a job," he added. "Job placement competition requires recruiters to only look at the highest-qualified candidates."

Holbrook's advice to young people interested in pursuing a career in business is straightforward. "Even if you have advanced degrees and multiple certifications, those alone will not guarantee success," he explained. "Your business relationship with others depends on your ability to be approachable and coachable." Holbrook also encourages young people

(*continued on the next page*)

(*continued from the previous page*)

**to develop a strong work ethic, be dependable with a sincere eagerness to please, and become the go-to person for difficult tasks. "Be prepared to work long hours to make an impression," he said.**

**"My education got me in the door," he added, "and my years of experience and understanding human behavior keep me working. If you love your work, the work has purpose in your life. If you strive to create the mature model of helping others with what you do, then you are rewarded beyond materialistic goals."**

# Financial Analyst

If you love numbers and keep close track of what the economy is doing on a daily basis, a financial analyst position may be a great choice. In this career, you will explore various investment portfolios and make sound predictions regarding what is going to happen financially to companies or industries. You won't spend all of your time poring over numbers and financial statements, however. A good amount of time will also be spent talking to and advising investors about stocks, bonds, earnings, pensions, and other finance-related subjects. You might work for a bank, an insurance company, or a corporation. Manisha Thakor, founder and CEO of MoneyZen Wealth Management, advises young people to gain as much work experience as they can while they take classes. In an interview with *U.S. News*, she stated, "Something as basic as offering to

Financial analysts do more than juggle numbers, of course. Often, they must also have a polished presentation and public speaking skills as well.

work with an established financial professional for five to ten hours a month can make all the difference." She also believes a key to professional success is found through networking and building relationships with the various people you meet along your journey. "So remember to keep one hand in the books, and one hand out shaking new ones."

- Expected job growth between now and 2020: 23 percent
- Possible spin-offs: risk analyst, fund manager, equity research analyst, real estate analyst

## Human Resources Manager

If you enjoy people more than numbers, a job in human resources management may work well for you. In this position, you act as the liaison between employees and managers. Strong communication skills will be needed as you juggle answering questions, making decisions, hiring and firing employees, organizing training sessions, evaluating performances, and negotiating conflicts. In an article from the *Princeton Review*, one human resources manager from a small firm explained, "You're the last line of defense between your company and confusion—and sometimes confusion wins."

- Expected job growth between now and 2020: 13 percent
- Possible spin-offs: employee relations manager, payroll manager, staffing manager

## Marketing Manager

If you're great at selling a product or service, marketing can be a compatible career pathway. As a marketing manager, you will create awareness of products and services for your employer. To do so, you have to be comfortable with all types of media, from television and radio to print and online. You will analyze the needs and interests of different target audiences, determining the best ways to persuade and influence them. This position calls on creativity, imagination, and even a bit of charm.

In an interview with job-resource site iSeek, Melanee Meagan described her job as marketing manager at Peace Coffee, a coffee roaster and wholesaler. She said, "I spend most of my time responding to requests for sponsorship, planning for events that are coming up, researching trends for future products, talking to roasters about how to describe our coffees, and continually updating our website, Facebook page, and Twitter account. Overall, I act as a conduit for sharing information about our company and making sure it is in a language that represents our vision and the mission of what we do."

She also offered advice to students interested in this type of work: "Find like-minded people in the field to talk with and ask questions. The field changes so quickly. There are always people trying to sell you things, and it's hard to know where to spend money. I think having a colleague group to share with is really valuable. It's like fact checking through conversations."

- Expected job growth between now and 2020: 14 percent
- Possible spin-offs: advertising manager, market development manager, marketing coordinator

## Training and Development Manager

If teaching others how to do things effectively and efficiently is one of your talents, you should consider pursuing a job as a training and development manager. In this role, you will identify training needs, direct courses,

# THE BEST BUSINESS SCHOOLS IN 2015

According to an annual report by *U.S. News*, these colleges are considered the best throughout the entire nation for their business programs. The schools average a full-time enrollment of 836 students. Of those who apply, anywhere from 6.8 to 43.8 percent are accepted into the schools.

| National Ranking | Name of School | F/T Enrollment | 2013–2014 Tuition | Percentage of Acceptance |
|---|---|---|---|---|
| 20 | Emory University Goizueta Business School | 352 | $46,000 | 31.2 |
| 19 | University of North Caroline—Chapel Hill Kenan-Flagler Business School | 573 | $31,510 in-state; $50,942 out of state | 43.8 |
| 18 | Carnegie Mellon University Tepper School of Business | 423 | $56,768 | 32 |
| 17 | Cornell University S.C. Johnson Graduate School of Management | 558 | $55,948 | 22.1 |
| 16 | University of California—Los Angeles Anderson School of Management | 724 | $48,711 in-state; $55,009 out of state | 22.3 |
| 15 | University of Texas—Austin McCombs School of Business | 511 | $33,298 in-state; $48,832 out of state | 32.6 |
| 14 | Duke University Fuqua School of Business | 861 | $55,300 | 26.5 |
| 13 | Yale University School of Management | 552 | $57,200 | 21.3 |

| National Ranking | Name of School | F/T Enrollment | 2013–2014 Tuition | Percentage of Acceptance |
|---|---|---|---|---|
| Tied for 11 | University of Virginia Darden School of Business | 633 | $48,402 in-state; $52,720 out of state | 25.1 |
| Tied for 11 | University of Michigan—Ann Arbor Stephen M. Ross School of Business | 941 | $52,200 in-state; $57,200 out of state | 33.7 |
| 10 | New York University Stern School of Business | 786 | $57,468 | 16 |
| 9 | Dartmouth College Tuck School of Business | 560 | $58,935 | 20.8 |
| 8 | Columbia University Business School | 1,279 | $60,720 | 18.1 |
| 7 | University of California—Berkeley Haas School of Business | 497 | $51,412 in-state; $53,959 out of state | 14.3 |
| 6 | Northwestern University Kellogg School of Management | 1,148 | $59,085 | 21.6 |
| 5 | Massachusetts Institute of Technology Sloan School of Management | 819 | $61,152 | 13.1 |
| 4 | University of Chicago Booth School of Business | 1,176 | $58,760 | 21 |
| Tied for 1 | University of Pennsylvania Wharton School | 1,677 | $59,736 | 18.7 |
| Tied for 1 | Stanford University Graduate School of Business | 809 | $59,550 | 6.8 |
| Tied for 1 | Harvard University Business School | 1,851 | $56,175 | 11.3 |

and improve the skills of others within a company. You will need to focus on critical thinking skills, public speaking techniques, and familiarity with a variety of teaching strategies. In a job description on the *Princeton Review* website, an article states, "Like anyone in the field of human resources, a training specialist is required to possess excellent interpersonal and communications skills and is expected to increase the skills, productivity, and quality of work among trainees. To achieve these goals," it continues, "training specialists plan, organize, and implement a wide range of training activities for both new hires and veteran employees. They conduct orientation sessions and arrange on-the-job training for new hires. They conduct workshops and arrange training for veteran employees, targeting skills that need

Teaching and training others who will benefit from your experience is an excellent way to combine your own skills in communication and education.

improving or helping them prepare for jobs requiring greater skill."
- Expected job growth between now and 2020: 14 percent
- Possible spin-offs: compensation and benefits manager, human resources manager, human resources specialist

## To MBA or Not to MBA?

Once your four years are over and you have a bachelor's degree in business, you might be asking yourself if you should keep going and earn a master's degree in business administration. It's not an easy question to answer. It means at least two more years of school, plus thousands of dollars. According to an article from the *Princeton Review*, however, for many business school students the effort is worth it: "The pay-off from higher salary to better career opportunities—is well worth the investment." The magazine suggests that any students considering going after a MBA ask themselves the following questions:

- *Are you sure you want to stay in a business career?* MBAs are for students who truly plan to spend their futures working in a business-related field, not those who just want a background in business for more general careers.
- *What are you hoping this additional education will help you accomplish?* Being able to provide a solid, strong answer to that question is a good indication you have given this some thought. You

might simply want to become knowledgeable in a new area, increase your chances of promotion within a company, or speed up your career path once you graduate.

- *If you want to change jobs or move into a different industry, is an MBA a requirement?* You might be able to accomplish the change by getting a much faster, much less expensive certificate.
- *Is now the best time to pursue your MBA?* Would waiting make more sense?

Give each question some serious thought. As the *Princeton Review* states, "You owe it to yourself to fully consider your options and weigh your concerns before leaping back into school."

# CHAPTER FIVE

# The Future of Business

There is no question that business is one field that is going to be around as long as people are. However, how and where business is conducted, what products and services are (and are not) in demand, and how you do your job on a daily basis are apt to be changing quickly and constantly.

What are the experts predicting for tomorrow's workplace? Tracey Wilen-Daugenti, author of *Society 3.0: How Technology Is Reshaping Education, Work, and Society*, believes there are several trends that will impact the way people work in the future.

- People will change jobs and employers far more often. Statistics indicate the average worker will have ten jobs during his or her work history.
- More workers will operate from home doing freelance or contract work. Meetings will be attended from home, at local cafes, or in hotel lobbies.
- As globalization increases, the need to know multiple languages will grow. "Our research indicates that employers predict a growing demand

In the future, as much work may well be done outside the workplace—for instance, at the local coffee shop—as inside it.

for workers who can do business in Spanish, Chinese, Russian and Arabic," says Caroline Molina Ray, executive director of research and publications at Apollo Research Institute.

- There will be less of a hierarchy of workers in future businesses, with the "high and mighty" boss inaccessible to the newbies and the entry-level workers. Wilen-Daugenti says, "Tomorrow's firms will be more interested in hearing ideas from everyone in an organization in order to harness the collective intelligence of all their employees and develop new innovations, better products and services."

# AN UNUSUAL OATH

In 2009, the graduates of the Thunderbird School of Global Management in Arizona listened to the usual commencement speeches, and then, led by school president Angel Cabrera, the graduates recited the following student-composed pledge, known as the Thunderbird Oath of Honor. According to the school, it reads:

"As a Thunderbird and a global citizen, I promise I will strive to act with honesty and integrity. I will respect the rights and dignity of all people. I will strive to create sustainable prosperity worldwide. I will oppose all forms of corruption and exploitation. And I will take responsibility for my actions. As I hold true to these principles, it is my hope that I may enjoy an honorable reputation and peace of conscience."

This focus on values and honesty may be a trend for a number of new business students. Applicants to Thunderbird are required to write an essay about the oath and what it means to them and their future in business.

# The Emphasis on "Soft Skills"

Many of the jobs in the field of business are on the rise, with strong growth projected for the next decade. In a personal interview, David Foote, Ph.D., the associate dean at Jones College of Business at Middle Tennessee State University, said, "Entrepreneurship and computer information systems related careers seem to be the ones toward which a great deal of attention is directed at present. Regardless of what jobs are most in demand, however, the typical business disciplines will remain relevant in some form." Foote went on to explain, "Businesses will still need people who make their names and products or services known and who bring in clients and customers (marketing); people who oversee the direction and functions of the businesses (management); people who manage and execute the financial activities and responsibilities of the businesses (finance), and who ensure compliance with regulatory agencies with regard to businesses' finances (accounting)."

Foote pointed out that currently there is a growing focus on the development of "soft skills" in business colleges. "No business will thrive, or perhaps even survive, without 'soft skills'—the ability to communicate effectively with others, the ability to build positive and productive relationships with one's coworkers and customers," he stated. "That array of skills is necessary for sustained success in any business, regardless of the specific product or service. Our business partners consistently tell us they can train new employees on the finer technical aspects of their jobs," added Foote, "but what they really look for in job applicants are the desire to work hard and the ability to work well with others. If you're a person who can 'play well in the sandbox with others,' you definitely have an advantage over those who can't." Because of this shift in emphasis, Jones College is working on adding "soft skills" to its core curriculum. "We like to think of Jones College as 'The College that Works,'" he explained. "We've got a lot of great things in process to make that happen."

# The Impact of Technology

There is no doubt that technology is going to impact the business world, just as it has done for the past few decades. Already workers can send documents, photographs, and videos instantly to any corner of the world and all for free. In countless ways, computers have revolutionized how daily business is done and will continue to do so in ways that still sound like they are straight out of a science fiction novel.

An article published in late 2013 in the *Telegraph* predicted that tomorrow's business offices might use hologram-like technology that will allow workers' images to appear almost like magic in virtual business meetings. Soon workers will sport wearable technology, computers that slip on their wrists or clothing to allow for constant communication wherever they are. All forms of communication will get faster, and, as the author of the article phrased it, these changes will present "immense opportunity for collaboration and new market development."

These expanding complex computer systems will become increasingly necessary as businesses focus more and more on globalization. According to an

As time goes by, technology such as the touch pad shown in use here will play an increasingly larger and important role in the world of business.

article in *Effect* magazine, the World Future Society, a group of highly educated experts on future trends, believes that globalization is the key to business success. "In order to survive, business owners and entrepreneurs will have to learn to look beyond their region or country of origin," it states. "To thrive, futurists predict businesses will need to work with suppliers, producers, and business partners from

# FASTEST-GROWING BUSINESS JOBS

The U.S. Bureau of Labor Statistics specializes in crunching numbers and making solid predictions about the future of jobs throughout the country. In 2013, it released its list of the thirty fastest-growing careers. How did business careers do? Out of the list, seven fell directly under the heading of business.

| Job | Projected Increase in 2016 | Education/Training Required |
|---|---|---|
| Network systems and data communications analysts | 53.4 percent | Associate's or bachelor's degree |
| Computer applications software engineers | 44.6 percent | Bachelor's degree with computer experience |
| Personal financial advisers | 41 percent | Bachelor's degree with additional training courses |
| Financial analysts | 33.8 percent | Bachelor's degree, with a master's recommended |
| Computer systems analysts | 29 percent | Bachelor's degree |
| Database administrators | 28.6 percent | Bachelor's degree in computer science and master's degree in business administration recommended |
| Computer software and systems software engineers | 28.2 percent | Bachelor's degree and computer experience |

other corners of the planet." Jim Rice, executive vice president of a Minneapolis-based health care consulting firm and a futurist adds, "Businesspeople are going to have to be citizens of the world . . . We live in a big world and businesses are going to have to learn to operate seamlessly within it."

Selling products and services to people who need them has been a part of the world's history since long before people knew how to write down prices and hand out receipts. It will continue long into the future when people stop using paper completely and every transaction will be stored somewhere in cyberspace. Business is an amazing field to explore and learn, from the entrepreneur creating something new for a dozen eager consumers to the executive analyst advising Fortune 500 CEOs on future investments. Start your exploration today and see what direction being in business can take you.

The future of business is exciting, strong, and changing. Where might you fit in?

# GLOSSARY

**accredited** Meeting the essential requirements of academic excellence.

**appraisal** An estimate of something's overall worth. Also, one person's evaluation of another.

**collaboration** Working with one or more people to create something.

**cybersecurity** Protection against harmful online/electronic data.

**defibrillator** A machine used to restart the heart via an electric shock.

**entrepreneurship** The process of starting a unique, new business.

**exploitation** Treating another person unfairly for personal gain.

**futurist** Someone who studies the future and makes educated predictions.

**globalization** The process of organizations spreading throughout the world.

**hierarchy** Ranking or organizing people based on status or authority.

**hologram** An image created by technology or computer software.

**impartial** Neutral, not belonging to any side.

**leukemia** A type of cancer affecting the bone marrow.

**macroeconomics** Economics dealing with the income/investments of a country as a whole.

**mediate** To guide disputes into a mutually agreeable conclusion.

**microeconomics** The branch of very special elements in economics.

**negotiate** To reach a compromise or agreement through discussion.

**nonprofit** A business intentionally designed not to gain money.

**template** Pattern or example to use.

**thrift shop** A business that sells discounted and/or previously owned items.

**virtual** Generated by a computer.

**viticulture** The study of grapes and the winemaking culture.

# FOR MORE INFORMATION

The Canadian Association of Business Students (CABS)
P.O. Box 266
Montreal, Succursale B
Montreal QB H3B 3J7
Canada
(514) 222-3064
Website: http://cabsonline.ca/en
CABS is a not-for-profit organization striving to provide
    leadership, support, and specialized services.

Canadian Federation of Independent Business
401-4141 Younge Street
Toronto, ON M2P2A6
Canada
(888) 234-2232
The Canadian Federation of Independent Business is
    the "big voice for small business," representing the
    interests of the small business community.

Mediation Training Institute International
5700 W. 79th Street
Prairie Village, KS 66208-4604
(888) 222-3271
Website: http://www.mediationworks.com
The Mediation Training Institute International teaches
    workers the skills of mediation and negotiation
    online and in person.

She Counts Inc.
P.O. Box 1063

Owings Mills, MD 21117
(410) 449-4475
Website: http://www.shecountsmed.org
She Counts offers programs and camps for young female
    entrepreneurs.

Small Business Bonfire
P.O. Box 3291
Allentown, PA 18106
(866) 944-4204
Website: http://smallbusinessbonfire.com
Small Business Bonfire is "where smart entrepre-
    neurs gather to spark change." Designed for small
    business owners who need a support network, it
    provides advice, tools, help, and resources.

U.S. Small Business Administration
409 3rd Street SW
Washington, DC 20416
(800) 827-5722
Website: http://www.sba.gov
The Small Business Administration offers free online
    courses, videos, chat sessions, and resource guides.

# Websites

Because of the changing nature of Internet links, Rosen
Publishing has developed an online list of websites
related to the subject of this book. This site is updated
regularly. Please use this link to access the list:

http://www.rosenlinks.com/RDFM/Busi

# FOR FURTHER READING

Baber, Anne. *Make Your Contacts Count: Networking Know-How for Business and Career Success.* New York, NY: AMACOM, 2007.

Canfield, Jack. *The Success Principles for Teens: How to Get from Where You Are to Where You Want to Be.* Deerfield Beach, FL: HCI, 2010.

Christen, Carol, and Richard Nolles. *What Color Is Your Parachute? For Teens.* Berkeley Hills, CA: Ten Speed Press, 2011.

Donovan, Sandy. *Job Smarts: How to Find Work or Start a Business, Manage Earnings, and More.* Minneapolis, MN: 21st Century, 2012.

Ferguson Publishing. *Business* (Careers in Focus). New York, NY: Ferguson Publishing, 2010.

Ferguson Publishing. *Business and Finance* (What Can I Do Now?). New York, NY: Ferguson Publishing, 2010.

Ferguson Publishing. *Business Managers* (Careers in Focus). New York, NY: Ferguson Publishing, 2009.

Ferguson Publishing. *Entrepreneurs* (Careers in Focus). New York, NY: Ferguson Publishing, 2009.

Ferguson Publishing. *Financial Services* (Careers in Focus). New York, NY: Ferguson Publishing, 2011.

Ferguson Publishing. *Professional Ethics and Etiquette.* New York, NY: Ferguson Publishing, 2009.

Ferguson Publishing. *Sales* (Careers in Focus). New York, NY: Ferguson Publishing, 2009.

Freedman, Hen. *Dream Jobs in Sports Management and Administration.* New York, NY: Rosen Publishing, 2012.

Harmon, Daniel. *Careers as a Marketing and Public Relations Specialist.* New York, NY: Rosen Publishing, 2014.

Ilasco, Meg Mateo. *Craft, Inc.: Turn Your Creative Hobby into a Business.* San Francisco, CA: Chronicle Books, 2009.

Jacobson, Ryan. *Get a Job at a Business.* Minneapolis, MN: Lerner Publishing Group, 2014.

Krause, Donald. *No Limit: The Texas Hold 'Em Guide to Winning in Business.* New York, NY: AMACOM, 2008.

Madson, Debbie. *Money Making Ideas for Kids and Teens: Starting Your Own Business: A Guide for Teen Entrepreneurs.* New York, NY: Amazon Digital Services, Inc., 2010.

Marlowe, Christie. *Presenting Yourself: Business Manners, Personality, and Etiquette.* Broomall, PA: Mason Crest, 2013.

Meyer, Susan. *Careers as a Bookkeeper and Auditor.* New York, NY: Rosen Publishing, 2014.

Swatz, Jon. *Young Wealth: Trade Secrets from Teens Who Are Changing American Business.* Bloomington, IN: Rooftop Publishing, 2006

# BIBLIOGRAPHY

ASCLA. "Thirty Most-Asked Questions About Small Business." American Library Association. Retrieved March 1, 2014 (http://www.ala.org/ascla/asclapubs/surviving/thirtymostasked/thirtymostasked).

Bergeron, Michelle. E-mail interview with author. March 14, 2014

Boyington, Briana. "Best Business Schools 2015." *U.S. News*, March 10, 2014. Retrieved March 14 2014 (http://www.usnews.com/education/best-graduate-schools/top-business-schools/slide-shows/best-business-schools-2015/1).

Brdve.net. "The Disadvantages of Distance Learning." Retrieved March 3, 2014 (http://www.brdve.net/disadvantages-of-distance-learning.php).

BusinessSchool Edge.com. "21 Business Skills Needed to Succeed." July 5, 2013. Retrieved March 11, 2014 (http://www.businessschooledge.com/21-business-skills-to-succeed).

Cheney, Alexandra. "A Career in Sales." *Wall Street Journal*, September 13, 2010. Retrieved March 5, 2014 (http://online.wsj.com/news/articles/SB10001424052748704206804575467963984089520).

Davie-Janes, Colleen. "A Day in the Life of an Administrative Assistant." Wall Street Services, March 20, 2014. Retrieved March 5, 2014 (http://www.wallstreetservices.com/day-in-the-life).

DeZube, Dona. "Seasonal Tax-Preparation Jobs." Monster.com. Retrieved March 14, 2014. (http://career-advice.monster.com/job-search/

company-industry-research/seasonal-tax-prepara
tion-jobs/article.aspx).

Fallon, Nicole. "9 Amazing Teen Entrepreneurs." Mother
Nature Network, September 9, 2013. Retrieved March
6, 2014 (http://www.mnn.com/family/family-activities/
stories/9-amazing-teen-entrepreneurs).

Foote, Daniel. E-mail interview with author. March
14, 2014.

Fox, Justin. "The Future of Work/Training Managers to Be-
have." *Time*, May 14, 2009. Retrieved March 17, 2014
(http://content.time.com/time/specials
/packages/article/0,28804,1898024_1898023_
1898084,00.html).

Haynie, Devon. "10 MBA Programs that Lead to Jobs."
*U.S. News*, March 11, 2014. Retrieved March
2, 2014 (http://www.usnews.com/education/
best-graduate-schools/the-short-list-grad-school/
articles/2014/03/11/10-mba-programs-that-lead-
to-jobs).

Holbrook, John. E-mail interview with author. March
13, 2014

iSeek Green. "Marketing Manager Interview."
Retrieved March 4, 2014 (http://www.iseek.org/
industry/green/careers/marketing-manager.html).

Jones, Phil. "How Evolving Technology Will Change
the Business World." *Telegraph*, September 11,
2013. Retrieved March 5, 2014 (http://www.
telegraph.co.uk/sponsored/technology/business-
technology/10298682/future-workplace-
technology.html).

Littlefield, Jamie. "Choosing the School for You."
About.com. Retrieved March 11, 2014 (http://

distancelearn.about.com/od/choosingaschool/a/
choosingaschool.htm).

McClaughy, Debra. E-mail interview with author.
March 17, 2014

Mediation Training Institute International. "Workplace
Mediator Certification." Retrieved March 9, 2014
(http://www.mediationworks.com/medcert3/
index.html).

Meyerson, Mitch. "10 Personality Traits of
Successful Business People." Mastering Online
Marketing. Retrieved March 7, 2014 (http://www
.masteringonlinemarketing.com/2012/03/10-
personality-traits-of-successful-business-people-2).

Monster. "In the Year 2016: The 30 Fastest-Growing
Jobs." Monster.com. Retrieved March 1, 2014
(http://www.boston.com/jobs/2013/12/23/
the-year-the-fastest-growing-jobs/GGDo2PVgihmp-
surdiPGUhO/story.html).

Online Education. "The Main Disadvantages of Internet
Learning." Bgiedu.net. Retrieved March 14,
2014 (http://www.bgiedu.net/the-main-
disadvantages-of-internet-learning.php).

Price, Jim. "10 Personality Traits Every Successful
Entrepreneur Has." *Business Insider*, February
15, 2013. Retrieved March 10, 2014 (http://
www.businessinsider.com/traits-of-successful-
entrepreneurs-2013-2).

*Princeton Review*. "Career: Human Resources Man-
ager/A Day in the Life of a Human Resources
Manager." Retrieved March 5, 2014 (http://www.
princetonreview.com/careers.aspx?cid=78).

*Princeton Review*. "Career: Training Specialist/A Day in the Life of a Training Specialist." Retrieved March 11, 2014 (http://www.princetonreview.com/careers.aspx?cid=182).

*Princeton Review*. "Is an MBA Right for You?" Retrieved March 8, 2014 (http://www.princeton review.com/business/pursuing-an-mba.aspx).

Rasmussen College. "2014 Business Career Outlook." Retrieved March 14, 2014 (http://www.rasmussen.edu/degrees/business/business-careers-guide).

Schroeder, Jacob. E-mail interview with author. March 16, 2014.

SheCounts. "A Teen's Guide to Starting a Successful Business." Retrieved March 13, 2014 (http://www.shecountsmd.org/teens-guide-starting-successful-business).

Stansberry, Glen. "10 Awesome Companies Built by Teens." American Express Open Forum, April 23, 2010. Retrieved March 11, 2014 (https://www.americanexpress.com/us/small-business/openforum/articles/10-awesome-companies-built-by-teens-1).

*U.S. News*. "Customer Service Representative: Reviews and Advice." Retrieved March 7, 2014 (http://money.usnews.com/careers/best-jobs/customer-service-representative/reviews).

*U.S.News*. "Financial Analyst." Retrieved March 7, 2014 (http://money.usnews.com/careers/best-jobs/financial-analyst).

Van Ausdell, Taryn. E-mail interview with author. March 15, 2014

# INDEX

# About the Author

Tamra Orr is the author of more than 350 nonfiction books for readers of all ages. She has a degree from Ball State University and lives in the Pacific Northwest with her husband and family. Orr created her writing business thirty years ago and now writes books, magazine articles, columns, and educational assessment materials. When she isn't writing or promoting her business, she loves to camp, read, write letters, and travel with her family.

# Photo Credits